The Effects of Praise

Andrew Wommack

© Copyright 2025 – Andrew Wommack

Printed in the United States of America. All rights reserved. No portion of this book may be reproduced, stored in a retrieval system, or transmitted in any form or by any means—electronic, mechanical, photocopy, recording, scanning, or other—except for brief quotations in critical reviews or articles, without the prior written permission of the publisher.

Unless otherwise indicated, all Scripture quotations are taken from the King James Version® of the Bible. Copyright © by the British Crown. Public domain.

Published by Andrew Wommack Ministries, Inc.

Woodland Park, CO 80863

ISBN 13 TP: 978-1-59548-751-3
ISBN 13 eBook: 978-1-6675-1163-4

For Worldwide Distribution, Printed in the USA

1 2 3 4 5 6 / 28 27 26 25

Contents

Introduction 1

Chapter 1 God is Worthy of Our Praise! 3
Chapter 2 Praise with Prayer 11
Chapter 3 Removing All Excuses 17
Chapter 4 Praise Is a Weapon 27
Chapter 5 Created for His Pleasure 35
Chapter 6 Stories of Blessing the Lord 45

Conclusion 51

Receive Jesus as Your Savior 54
Receive the Holy Spirit 56
Call for Prayer 58
About the Author 59

Would you like to get more out of this teaching?

Scan the QR code to access this teaching in video or audio formats to help you dive even deeper as you study.

Accessing the teaching this way will help you get evenmore out of this booklet.

awmi.net/browse

Introduction

There is a popular song today that includes this line: "I raise a hallelujah, my weapon is a melody." It's true that praise to God is a weapon against the enemy, but praise is so much more than that! Praise is a huge subject. Much of the book of Psalms is devoted to this topic. I could never cover all that the Word of God has to say about it, but what I will explain will help you in every situation.

You may not have considered this, but your praise life reflects how spiritually healthy you are. It's like taking your spiritual pulse. If you aren't constantly praising and thanking God, you are spiritually unhealthy.

In the Scriptures, you'll find that praise is a common trait in people who have a close relationship with God. Many of these people faced terrible situations—much worse than you or I are probably in right now—and yet they were able to praise God. It just goes to show that praising God is a choice, and it is not dependent on our circumstances.

In this booklet, I will be explaining how praise affects you, how it affects the devil, and how it affects God. When you praise God, each of these effects will benefit you. Most people have never realized that praise benefits them. They look at it as only benefitting God. Now, it's true that praise does benefit Him, but there are other benefits that you'll experience once you renew your mind to these truths and apply them.

This is one of the most foundational teachings the Lord has ever given to me. It is absolutely essential to having a Christian life that's healthy and thriving. Get ready to discover the effects of praise. You are going to be blessed!

Chapter 1

God is Worthy of Our Praise!

Have you ever considered that you can praise God in every situation? I didn't say *for* every situation. You may not be able to look at every area of your life and find it praiseworthy, but you can always be praising and thanking God. Why? Because God is always worthy of praise.

As the psalmist wrote, *"Oh that* men *would praise the* Lord for *his goodness, and for his wonderful works to the children of men!"* (Ps. 107:8)

God's goodness is undeniable, and His worthiness of our praise is absolute. This alone is reason enough to praise Him morning, noon, and night. However, when we praise God, it benefits us, which brings me to the first effect of praise that I want to share with you: Praising God positively affects our spiritual, emotional, and physical well-being.

When we praise God, it reminds us that He is our source and greater than all of our problems. When we praise, we are ushered into His presence where there is *"fullness of joy"* (Ps. 16:11), and this joy is our strength (Neh. 8:10). Instead of ruining our health with stress and anxiety, we can focus all of our love and attention on God, and it will produce peace (Isa. 26:3) and a merry heart, which *"doeth good* like *a medicine"* (Prov. 17:22).

Most importantly, praising God cultivates intimacy with Him, and through this intimate relationship, we become fully persuaded of His great love for us. When trials come, instead of grumbling and getting into fear, we choose to continue to praise Him and *"count it all joy"* (James 1:2).

Rejoice in the Lord Always!

Did you know that praising God is a choice? It's true, and it is not based on having circumstances that are always pleasant. Let's look at the Apostle Paul for example. He was in a worse situation than most people have ever been in, and yet he still praised God. There is a lesson to learn from this. In Philippians 4:4, he wrote,

Rejoice in the Lord alway: and again I say, Rejoice.

I believe that the reason Paul repeated the word "*rejoice*" is because a lot of people wouldn't have believed him. They'd say, "Well, he couldn't have meant what he said. You can't rejoice if you've had a death in the family, are going through a divorce, or if you've lost your job." But, no, Paul repeated himself to emphasize that he meant for us to rejoice always.

Notice also that Paul, writing under the inspiration of the Holy Spirit, is saying this as a command from God. Again, this underscores that rejoicing is something you can choose to do, despite what may be going on in your life. So, as you're reading, I want to encourage you to let God's Word be true and every man a liar (Rom. 3:4). What Paul is saying applies to you today. You *can* rejoice at all times, in all circumstances, in any situation.

Joy vs. Rejoice

The truth is that in your born-again spirit, you not only have joy, but you also have love, peace, and more!

> *But the fruit of the Spirit is love, joy, peace, longsuffering, gentleness, goodness, faith, meekness, temperance.*
>
> Galatians 5:22-23a

That doesn't mean you always have joy in your soul. You may not be *feeling* happy, but you do have joy in your spirit.

However, to experience this joy, you must start rejoicing. I've had to do this many times, sometimes through gritted teeth. In my physical, emotional realm, I was hurting. But I decided that I was going to praise God. When I did that, it was powerful. I began to be uplifted. Joy began springing up in my soul.

Years ago, just after my wife Jamie and I had come home late from an overseas trip, we got a call from my oldest son Joshua that my youngest son Peter had died. I said, "Don't let anybody touch him until we get there." Jamie and I immediately began to pray, and then we got up, got dressed, and started the hour-long drive into Colorado Springs. During the trip, I started having the same emotions that you would have if you were told that your son was dead. I was tempted to yield to feelings of grief and sorrow, but I knew that Scripture said to rejoice in the Lord always. By this time in my Christian walk, I had made the decision that I was not going to gripe and complain about anything. I wasn't going to focus on the negative. Now, I'm not critical of anybody who grieves over the loss of someone. I understand. Like I said, I felt those emotions. But

I'm saying that I knew I still had the choice to rejoice. It would've been the wrong response for me to start voicing my feelings.

So, I decided I was going to rejoice in the Lord. I was not going to let grief or bitterness overwhelm me. Now, remember, I didn't have joy in my emotions, but I knew I had it in my spirit. So, I began to say, "*I will bless the Lord at all times: his praise* shall *continually* be *in my mouth*" (Ps. 34:1).

Rejoicing is an action; it's not a feeling. Out of your mouth, you can say, "Father, I love You. I praise You. You are a good God." This is what I started doing after I heard that my son was dead! You might think that's weird, but I think you're weird if you're just sitting there dealing with your problems as if there wasn't a God. You can rejoice always.

When I started praising God, it just primed the pump on the inside of me. Suddenly, the power of God came upon me. Faith rose up. This is what Colossians 2:7 says will happen when you begin to give thanks unto God. Then God started bringing to my remembrance prophecies about Peter that hadn't yet come to pass. It just clicked inside me—that meant my son had to live!

I went from feeling no joy whatsoever to actually laughing. I praised myself happy. I got so excited that I looked over at Jamie and said, "This is going to be the greatest miracle we've ever seen!"

When we got to Colorado Springs, Joshua came rushing out to meet us and said, "Dad, I don't know what happened, but five or ten minutes after I called you, Peter just sat up and started talking." He had been dead for over four hours and had been stripped naked, fitted with a toe tag, and put in a cooler in a morgue. We went in to see him, and he was talking, totally coherent, and there was no brain damage. It was just awesome! All of this happened because of the power of praise.

Perhaps you're not praising God because you're waiting for the situation to turn around or your feelings to change. Anybody can rejoice after everything works out. But I'm telling you, it's a greater demonstration of faith to praise God when you've just heard bad news and it looks like destruction is upon you. When you start praising God in the midst of the storm, that's what sets you apart as spiritually mature.

Set-Free Mindset

You've got to get free from the mindset that validates reasons for being depressed and discouraged. Psychology has done a tremendous amount of damage to society by saying that in some circumstances, you just can't help but act according to your feelings. It says that if you don't, you're in denial. But, no, Paul said to rejoice in the Lord always (Phil. 4:4).

Even though some religious groups today teach that you should go around feeling miserable when bad things happen, remember that when Paul said to rejoice, he was writing from prison. He was living in an ungodly government system that was openly hostile to Christians. Nero, the emperor, was evil, professing himself to be God. He ruled with absolute authority, and yet in that situation, Paul talked about joy and rejoicing over fifteen times throughout the book of Philippians. It's his happiest book. If he could rejoice in his situation, you can too.

Some people might take offense to what I'm saying: "You mean there are *no* exceptions for being depressed and discouraged?" Well, you have a choice, and until you can accept responsibility and recognize that you are more than an animal, just responding to instinct and stimuli, you will always be a victim and not a victor. All Satan has to do is bring some problem across your path, and you'll fall apart. But you were created in the image of God. You have a choice. You don't have to be captive to your emotions.

It's your soul that fluctuates based on your circumstances: It'll go from encouraged to discouraged and back again. That's why the Scripture says,

> *Bless the Lord, O my soul: and all that is within me, bless his holy name.*
>
> Psalm 103:1

You have to take authority over your soul and say, "I *will* rejoice in the Lord always." Don't give yourself any excuses: your spouse, your boss, or the color of your skin; *choose* to praise God—He is worthy!

Chapter 2

Praise with Prayer

Did you know that you should not be praying about your problem unless you do it with thanksgiving? Most people don't believe that. They think of prayer as their opportunity to complain, express their unbelief, and inform "poor, misinformed" God about how bad their situation is. Then they wonder why they're not getting better results in prayer. I tell you, there is a better way to pray!

Paul wrote in Philippians 4:6,

Be careful for nothing; but in every thing by prayer and supplication with thanksgiving let your requests be made known unto God.

The word "*careful*" here means not to be anxious. Paul was saying not to worry about anything. Now, many people will say, "I don't want to worry," but they'll have a whole list of reasons why they feel they're justified in worrying. No, worrying is a choice!

You know, when people say, "Well, take care," my response—usually under my breath—is to say, "For nothing." I am not going to take care. I am not going to worry. I'm going to cast all of my care upon the Lord because He cares for me (1 Pet. 5:7).

The Sandwich Technique

The Lord wants to hear what's on your heart. The Lord wants you to bring your problems to Him, but how you do it is even more important than what you pray. The Scripture says,

> *Enter into his gates with thanksgiving,* and *into his courts with praise: be thankful unto him,* and *bless his name.*
>
> Psalm 100:4

When Jesus was teaching about how to pray, He said,

Our Father which art in heaven, Hallowed be thy name. Thy kingdom come. Thy will be done in earth, as it is in heaven. Give us this day our daily bread. And forgive us our debts, as we forgive our debtors. And lead us not into temptation, but deliver us from evil: For thine is the kingdom, and the power, and the glory, for ever. Amen.

Matthew 6:9b-13

Notice that Jesus started the prayer with praise and then ended it with praise. Any request you have should be slipped between the two slices of praise. It's what I call a "sandwich technique." Somebody will ask, "What does having this model for prayer do?" First of all, it gives you the proper context and perspective on prayer that most people totally miss. The second thing it'll do is shrink your problems down to where you'll realize they're no big deal for God.

If you would praise God and "*be careful for nothing, but in every thing by prayer and supplication with thanksgiving let your requests be made known unto God*" (Phil. 4:6), it would radically transform your life and the way you see your prayers answered. Praise is one of the most important things that you can do. Don't ever pray without praise!

Supernatural Peace

Perhaps you find yourself unable to sleep at night because you take your problems to bed with you. Even when you do sleep, your dreams may be full of your fears or failures. This is happening because you are violating this principle of being careful for nothing (Phil. 4:6). You're not casting all your care upon the Lord (1 Pet. 5:7). I am not saying this to condemn you; I'm saying it to help you experience God's peace. The Scripture says,

> *Thou wilt keep* him *in perfect peace,* whose *mind is stayed on* thee: *because he trusteth in thee.*
>
> Isaiah 26:3

If you want to experience perfect peace, you must trust that God is greater than your problems, and then let Him bear all the care and concern of them while you keep your mind on Him. Otherwise, prayer laden with care, which is unbelief, will do you no good. When you cast your cares on the Lord (1 Pet. 5:7), Scripture says,

> *the peace of God, which passeth all understanding, shall keep your hearts and minds through Christ Jesus.*
>
> Philippians 4:7

I know that a lot of people will struggle to understand how they could have peace when their circumstances haven't changed. But God's supernatural peace isn't related to what's happening in your circumstances. It's not logical;

it goes beyond your understanding and keeps your heart and mind at ease in the midst of your situation. I can tell you that I have done what the Word says, and I have had a supernatural peace from God come over me. When you give your care to God, He gives you His peace in exchange.

On our website, we have testimony after testimony of people who have cast their cares on the Lord and then experienced this peace that I'm talking about. People around them—their family, friends, and doctors—thought they were in denial. Some even got mad at them. But because these people did what Philippians 4:4-7 says, they had a peace from God that passed understanding, and things worked out.

Here's the bottom line: Before taking your requests to the Lord, start by thanking and praising Him. Cast your cares upon Him by acknowledging that He is greater than any problem you could ever face. If you do this, you will experience His supernatural peace and greatly improve your prayer results.

Chapter 3

Removing All Excuses

God holds us responsible for rejoicing and praising Him and being thankful for all the good things He's given us. I don't know anyone who gets up in the morning and thinks, *Today I'm going to be unthankful.* Everybody understands that being thankful and praising God are better than griping and complaining. However, for most people, expressing gratitude to God is contingent on their daily experiences or current circumstances. They are more inclined to praise when life goes well, but during difficult times, their motivation decreases. If things take a turn for the worse, they feel justified in withholding praise, believing they have not wronged Him. Their praise is driven solely by their emotions, and that's not the way it's supposed to be.

Look at Deuteronomy 28:45-48:

Moreover all these curses shall come upon thee, and shall pursue thee, and overtake thee, till thou be destroyed; because thou hearkenedst not unto the voice of the Lord *thy God, to keep his commandments and his statutes which he commanded thee: And they shall be upon thee for a sign and for a wonder, and upon thy seed for ever. Because thou servedst not the Lord thy God with joyfulness, and with gladness of heart, for the abundance of* all *things; Therefore shalt thou serve thine enemies which the* Lord *shall send against thee, in hunger, and in thirst, and in nakedness, and in want of all* things: *and he shall put a yoke of iron upon thy neck, until he have destroyed thee.*

Let me be clear: The curses described in this passage are part of the Old Covenant. They would come upon anyone who didn't obey God. Praise God that Jesus became a curse for us so that we might be blessed (Gal. 3:13-14). As New Covenant believers, we will not experience this wrath and punishment associated with sin. Nonetheless, the principle is valid. It shows *why* God brought this curse upon the Israelites.

You see, it doesn't please the Lord when we don't serve Him "*with joyfulness and …gladness of heart, for the abundance of all things*" (Deut. 28:47). God would have been unjust to punish them for not being joyful and thankful if they were unable to do it. The very fact that He is holding them accountable, and even bringing judgment upon them if they don't praise Him, shows that this is not optional.

You are responsible for your emotions. You might respond by saying, "Andrew, all you're doing is heaping more guilt and condemnation upon me and making me feel worse." That is not my intent. However, you will never break out of the cycle of going by your feelings if you don't recognize that God's command to praise Him means that you *can* do it.

Be of Good Cheer!

These things I have spoken unto you, that in me ye might have peace. In the world ye shall have tribulation: but be of good cheer; I have overcome the world.

John 16:33

On the night before His crucifixion, Jesus was speaking to His disciples and He warned them that in the world, they would have tribulation. Immediately after that, He told them to be of good cheer. He wasn't telling them to rejoice because their lives were going to be free of problems and troubles. As a matter of fact, shortly after He made that statement, the disciples would go through the greatest trial of their lives seeing Jesus taken captive and then crucified. Nevertheless, He told them, "*Be of good cheer; I have overcome the world*" (John 16:33b).

Notice that Jesus didn't say He was *going* to overcome the world. No, He had already overcome the world. Whatever you're going through, it's already been overcome. If you're facing a death sentence or some incurable disease, God has already overcome it. If you're facing a divorce, God has already overcome the rejection, the hurt, and the pain of it. He bore all of these things for you. Now He's telling you to be of good cheer. Again, this is a command.

I know that the tendency for most Christians is to resist what I'm saying. They think, *Well, you just don't understand my situation.* Believe me: God does. The Bible says,

> *For we have not an high priest which cannot be touched with the feeling of our infirmities; but was in all points tempted like as* we are, yet *without sin.*
> Hebrews 4:15

God has experienced everything you're experiencing. The primary reason most people don't praise God is because they are focused on what Satan is trying to do in their lives instead of being focused on what God has done for them. But God's supply is greater than your need. Whatever it is that's coming against you, God has already overcome it. You need to understand how much He has done for you.

Just a Light Affliction

To help put things in perspective, I want to share some of what the Apostle Paul experienced. Some people think that the only reason he was able to issue this command to rejoice always was because he didn't have any problems. As evidence, they look at 2 Corinthians 4:17 where Paul wrote that he suffered a light affliction. Well, let me just share with you a little about Paul's "light" affliction.

In comparison to those who called themselves apostles but were false, he wrote that he had taken stripes above measure (2 Cor. 11:23). That means he had been whipped so many times that he had lost count. How many Christians today can say that? Then, in the same verse, Paul said he had been in prisons more frequently. You might have been in prison for doing something wrong, but Paul had been unjustly imprisoned for preaching the Gospel. This was persecution. And if what he was experiencing wasn't bad enough, he finished the verse by saying he faced death often. Not many Christians can say they face death on a regular basis. Let me just run through the rest of this list Paul gives:

> *Of the Jews five times received I forty stripes save one. Thrice was I beaten with rods, once was I stoned, thrice I suffered shipwreck, a night and a day I have been in the deep; In journeyings often, in perils of waters, in perils of robbers, in perils by mine own countrymen, in perils by the heathen, in perils in the city, in perils in the wilderness, in perils in the sea, in perils among false brethren; In weariness and painfulness, in watchings often, in hunger and thirst, in fastings often, in cold and nakedness. Beside those things that are without, that which cometh upon me daily, the care of all the churches.*
> 2 Corinthians 11:24-28

Nobody today has suffered the way Paul suffered. This is what he called his light affliction. Now, if his affliction was light and yet his sufferings were greater than yours or mine, how can we justify talking about how heavy our afflictions are? The truth is, we have no excuse. If Paul could rejoice always, then we can too!

Heaven Is Going to Be a Blast

Think about it: The worst thing that could happen to you is that you would die and go be with the Lord. When you understand this, it causes you to rejoice. Like Jesus, the Apostle Paul was also facing imminent death by the time he wrote the book of Philippians. But he was actually excited:

For to me to live is *Christ, and to die* is *gain. But if I live in the flesh, this* is *the fruit of my labour: yet what I shall choose I wot not. For I am in a strait betwixt two, having a desire to depart, and to be with Christ; which is far better: Nevertheless to abide in the flesh* is *more needful for you. And having this confidence, I know that I shall abide and continue with you all for your furtherance and joy of faith; That your rejoicing may be more abundant in Jesus Christ for me by my coming to you again.*

Philippians 1:21-26

Paul, even in a situation where he was unjustly accused and in prison, was rejoicing in the Lord. He understood this truth that the worst thing that could happen to him was that he would die and go be with Jesus.

We sing these songs about going to heaven and what a day it will be. Then, if the doctor tells us we're going there, many of us will start crying like it's the end of the world. There's a disconnect there. If heaven is so wonderful, why not reach up and kiss the doctor and say, "That's awesome! Today I could see Jesus! My faith could become sight!"?

Now, people will say, "You've lost your mind." Well, actually, I *have* lost my mind. I have the mind of Christ now (1 Cor. 2:16). I'm looking at things as Jesus did. The Bible says that for the joy set before Him, He endured the cross, despising the shame (Heb. 12:2). Jesus and Paul had the attitude that you need to have. It doesn't happen overnight, but if you start renewing your mind (Rom. 12:2), you'll begin looking at your circumstances through Jesus' eyes more and more.

Heaven is going to be a blast! There will be no more sickness, sorrow, or pain. Now, I don't believe we have to die sick, poor, and defeated. When we are satisfied (Ps. 91:16), we should just give up the ghost and go. If we never see our healing manifest, it shouldn't stop us from rejoicing. We can still rejoice that we are soon going to be out of our physical bodies and in glorified ones. The former things won't even come to mind (Isa. 65:17). We won't even remember them.

I believe that it's God's will for you to prosper financially, but if your faith never worked the way it should have and you never saw financial prosperity in your life, you are going to live forever in a mansion that God has built for you (John 14:2). You should still be able to rejoice because you are going to live in splendor throughout all eternity. If you win, you win, and if you lose, you win because of Jesus. You can't lose for winning. Praise God!

Chapter 4

Praise Is a Weapon

Not everything that happens is the result of natural and logical circumstances. There is a devil, and he is behind a lot of the evil we see in our world. Many people—even some Christians—believe that sickness is merely a physical problem. You can tell by how they deal with sickness: Their default is to go to the doctor and resort to modern medicine to seek healing. I'm not saying there's anything wrong with that if they're doing it in faith. But if you read the New Testament, Jesus cast demons out of people to heal blindness, deafness, and even curvature of the spine. I'm not saying that everything that happens is demonic. But a lot of it is.

Some people don't realize that they have an Enemy who is attacking them. Jesus said that the thief—Satan—comes to steal, to kill, and to destroy (John 10:10). The devil is a spiritual being, so how do you fight an adversary you can't see or touch? Most people don't realize that praise is a powerful weapon against him. He cannot stand praise. This is the second effect of praise I want to share with you.

Praise = Strength

Jesus equated praise with strength. This is an important truth that most people overlook when they read what He told the chief priests:

> *Have ye never read, Out of the mouth of babes and sucklings thou hast perfected praise?*
>
> Matthew 21:16b

This is a quotation from Psalm 8:2, which says,

> *Out of the mouth of babes and sucklings hast thou ordained strength because of thine enemies, that thou mightest still the enemy and the avenger.*

Notice that there are a couple of words Jesus changed. That doesn't mean He violated what the psalmist wrote; it just means He provided commentary on what was written. If you put these two verses together, you'll get a more complete revelation of what God intended. Do you see that Jesus changed "*ordained strength*" (Ps. 8:2) to "*perfected praise*"

(Matt. 21:16)? By putting these two together, you can say that praise is strength. This is a powerful truth! Nehemiah confirmed this when he said, "*The joy of the Lord is your strength*" (Neh. 8:10). Joy strengthens you against the Enemy. If you're weak today, then offer up praise to God, and you'll begin to have strength.

Praise Stills the Avenger

Did you know that when you operate in praise, it stops Satan from advancing on you? It's like God puts a force field around you: He goes before you and behind you (Isa. 52:12). Satan just can't gain an inroad into you.

The latter part of Psalm 8:2 says that God has ordained strength that He might "*still the enemy and the avenger.*" The scripture doesn't give a full explanation of how this works, but here's the way I see it: Satan wanted to be like the Most High (Isa. 14:14). His transgression against God wasn't that he hated God; He envied Him. He wanted the worship and praise and glory that went to God alone. Satan literally tried to overthrow God and assume His position. So, God kicked him out of heaven. But the one thing he still craves is the praise of God.

When we praise God, we are denying Satan the one thing that he has always wanted. It's like putting salt in an open wound. That's why he's so averse to it. If you put this idea together with Psalm chapter 22, where it says, "*But thou* art *holy,* O thou *that inhabitest the praises of Israel*" (Ps. 22:3), then it paints this picture that when we praise God, His presence manifests. The presence, the anointing, and the power of God will halt the devil in his tracks!

I'm sure you've been around somebody who thinks they're better than everybody else. They can't endure others getting attention. Even when others start talking about what's going on in their lives, these people will interrupt them and try to divert the attention back to themselves. If they can't monopolize the conversation, they'll just leave. They won't stick around to see other people get attention or credit for anything. They'll always need to be the center of everything. Well, Satan is like that. He's an egomaniac. When you go to praising God, it literally drives him crazy!

Satan will do all he can to get your praise: He'll try to divert your attention to your problems or yourself. You've got to be conscious of this when you're going through trials. Don't give him what he wants. Even if you say nothing at all, that would be better than giving your praise to him.

Distractions from the Devil

One of the reasons Santa Claus and the Easter Bunny are so popular today is that Satan uses them to take praise and worship away from God. He'd rather we focus on a fat man in a red suit and a rabbit that lays eggs. Some of these things don't even make sense. But the devil will do anything to distract us from Jesus' birth and resurrection. For many, it's working: Christians celebrate the pagan meanings for these holidays rather than the godly meanings behind them. We need to remember that they were meant for the praise and worship of the Lord.

I am not saying that if you have anything to do with Santa Claus or an Easter bunny, or if you dress up at Halloween, you're of the devil. But Satan's worst lies are always the ones that seem good on the surface. They always resemble the truth.

Originally, Halloween, for instance, was a godly holiday. It means "All Hallows' Eve." It was the evening before All Saints' Day when you took time to remember the godly people and the contributions they had made. It was a holy evening. Then, of course, Satan came along and put in witches and goblins. Now people are more excited about dressing up and getting candy. Today, it's pretty easy to recognize all of the demonic symbolism associated with Halloween, but that isn't the case with Easter or Christmas.

Easter was a time set aside to commemorate the death, burial, and resurrection of the Lord Jesus Christ. But instead of worshiping Him, many people decorate eggs and have their kids hunt for them in their yards. Many of these same people will dress up in fancy clothes on Easter Sunday and go to church. Now, while there's nothing wrong with either one of these in their place, if that's all Easter has become for you, that's what Satan intended. The resurrection of Jesus should be more exciting than any of these things!

Of course, Christmas is meant to celebrate God being with us and the gift of His Son coming to redeem us. It's all about the advent of the Lord Jesus. And yet for many people, it's about presents and a jolly man flying around on a reindeer-pulled sleigh who supposedly can cover the whole world in one night and dispense toys to everybody. Now, again, I'm not condemning anybody for celebrating Christmas this way. But we need to make sure that we're worshiping God in spirit and in truth (John 4:24). It's worship free from the devil's distractions.

Praise When Under Attack

If you are under attack by the Enemy, one of the greatest things you can do is begin to praise God. It's one of the ways you resist the devil (James 4:7b). The devil will have to flee from you.

If there was no other benefit to praising God than aggravating the devil, it would be well worth it. For all of the problems that he's caused you and your family, for all the problems he may be causing you now, he shouldn't get your praise too. You've got a weapon against him. Start using it. Praising God in the middle of a difficult situation will confuse the devil. He'll have to give up and turn tail. Praise has a powerful effect on the devil. If you're going through a hard time, just start praising God!

Chapter 5

Created for His Pleasure

The most important reason to praise God is because of how it ministers to the Lord. Sad to say, most Christians have never really thought about how praise affects God. We tend to think that the only thing He really values is our service. But, no, God didn't create us to serve Him, even though that's important. He created us for relationship. And did you know that relationship was designed to be mutually beneficial? This means our relationship with God gives Him something He needs and truly desires. You might be thinking, *What do I have to give God?* I want to look at a story in Acts 13 that I believe will answer this question.

Minister to the Lord

Paul, Silas, and other men were in the church at Antioch, and the Scripture says,

> *As they ministered to the Lord, and fasted, the Holy Ghost said, Separate me Barnabas and Saul for the work whereunto I have called them.*
>
> Acts 13:2

One day as I read this verse, the words "*they ministered to the Lord*" just jumped off the page! I thought, *How do you minister to the Lord?* That's an important question.

Some people think, *Well, as we serve Him by sharing the Gospel and meeting the needs of others, we are ministering to the Lord.* I don't discount that. It is certainly one of the ways to minister to Him. When Jesus told His disciples how they had met the needs of others, He said,

> *Inasmuch as ye have done it unto one of the least of these my brethren, ye have done* it *unto me.*
>
> Matthew 25:40

But at Antioch, these men weren't ministering to anyone in this way. And yet the Bible says they ministered to the Lord. Amazing! I concluded that there must be more to ministering to the Lord than what would typically come to mind. The answer goes back to the question about what we have to offer God: It's our praise!

You see, all that Paul, Silas, and the others were doing was worshiping God, thanking Him for all the good things He had done, and fasting. Did you know that this ministered to the Lord? This brings me to the third and most important effect of your praise: Praise ministers to and brings pleasure to God.

Created for God's Pleasure

God's original purpose for everything He created might shock you. It says, in Revelation 4:11,

Thou art worthy, O Lord, to receive glory and honour and power: for thou hast created all things, and for thy pleasure they are and were created.

This is powerful! Notice the wording that "*for thy pleasure they are and were created.*" In other words, it was God's original purpose for all things to give Him pleasure, and it's still His purpose.

Very few people have moved into a relationship with God where they understand that God gets pleasure from *them*, not just what they do. Did you know that God just loves you and that He wants a relationship with you? Of course, He wants your service too, but it is not a substitute for relationship with Him. Just like your own children bring you pleasure, even if they have disappointed you or rebelled against you, your Father is pleased with you when you praise Him, even in bad situations.

Can you imagine if a parent was only pleased with their kids when they mowed the lawn, washed the dishes, or cleaned their rooms? That would be a bad parent. However, if you were to take a poll among Christians, most of them would say they don't think God is very pleased with them. They've never pictured God as a loving Father. But just like you love watching your children play, grow up, and learn new things, so does your Father in heaven (Matt. 7:11)!

God Needs Love

God is love (1 John 4:8). He doesn't just have love for us; love is the core of His being. Any person who loves has a need to be loved in return. Why? Because unrequited love is heartbreaking. We've probably all experienced it. So, in this sense, God needs us. I'm not saying that God has a weakness or that He's inadequate in any way. He's not insufficient without our love, but He created us for His pleasure, to praise and worship Him. I believe it grieves Him when we are not living our purpose. As I mentioned in the last chapter, God inhabits our praises (Ps. 22:3). That means He lives in our praises. It actually blesses Him. It's a big part of our relationship with Him.

More than what you can do for Him, God wants your heart. If He gets your heart, He will have your service. Service should be the byproduct of relationship with God, not a substitute for relationship with God.

Religion has made people become so focused on doing things. Many of us have become human doings instead of human beings. We go out and do a work for God and totally skip over relationship with Him. When we believe that our purpose is to accomplish things, we miss the most important thing of all.

The Original Justification for Man's Existence

I attended a missions conference where a man spoke about our responsibility to minister to other people. He said, "The sole justification for your existence on this earth is to lead another person to the Lord." While I understood the point he was making, and even agreed with it to a degree, the Lord spoke to me, "What was the justification for Adam and Eve's existence before the Fall? Who were they going to lead into salvation?" You know, there was no possible way they could have justified their existence since there were no lost people to evangelize, no sick people to heal, and no poor people to bless financially. Therefore, Adam and Eve's purpose couldn't have involved some kind of service for God.

On top of all that, they didn't have any physical needs to pray about, no need for emotional healing, and no sins to confess. And yet for most Christians, if you could distill their relationship down to its simplest form, the extent of their relationship with God doesn't go beyond praying for their needs. Or, if they're really spiritual, they also pray for the needs of others. But what would you pray about if you knew all your needs were met?

Did you know that God has anticipated every need you could ever have and has already blessed you with every spiritual blessing in Christ Jesus (Eph. 1:3)? Now it's just a matter of renewing your mind to understand what God has provided in the spiritual realm and then making it manifest in the physical realm by faith. The Bible gives you a window into the spiritual realm so that you can see what has been provided. When you believe God's promises, your faith brings what He has already done out of the spiritual realm and into the physical realm for you to enjoy.

Before they sinned, Adam and Eve were living in this reality where God had already made provision for everything. So, what did their relationship with Him look like? I believe it looked like them telling God, "Today was amazing! We found new trees! We tasted fruit we never tasted before. We saw an animal that looked like it was made up of leftover parts from other animals: It had a duck's bill, a beaver's tail, and an otter's feet! It was awesome! Thank You for what You've done!" Adam and Eve were just praising God, thanking Him, and expressing their wonder at His creation. And, again, not only was it the original justification for man's existence; it still is today (Rev. 4:11).

You were created for God's pleasure. You were made to be an object of God's love. God loves you just for who you are. If you were the only person on the face of the earth, I believe that Jesus would have died for you. If there was nothing for you to do for Him, God would love you. If you can believe that, then you also need to believe that He needs your love in return. He wants you to praise and thank Him, just like those men were doing in Acts 13. They actually ministered to God! I believe that one of the greatest things about praise is how it touches God's heart. And it's something you can do anywhere, any time of the day. Just take a moment right now to thank God for how good He is!

Paul and Silas

I want to share another example from the life of Paul because he's such a great example of everything I've been sharing. In Acts 16, Paul had a vision where a man told him,

Come over into Macedonia, and help us.
Acts 16:9b

Paul and Silas traveled to Philippi, one of the country's major cities, and when they came across a young slave girl with a spirit of divination, Paul cast the spirit out of her. Now, this girl had made her masters a lot of money from her fortune telling, but when she was delivered of the demon and their hope of more profit was lost, they were really upset. They were able to stir up the magistrates and have Paul and Silas severely beaten and then imprisoned! It says they were put in the inner cell, the darkest part of the prison. Mind you, this wasn't like the prisons that we have today. There weren't flat-screen televisions, internet access, or exercise yards. The conditions of these places were harsh.

Now, picture this: You've traveled to a country at the word of the Lord, to help people, and you wind up in a situation where you're unjustly prosecuted and flogged and then thrown in a dungeon. The last thing most Christians would be doing is praising and thanking God, especially knowing He led them to their situation. I guarantee they'd be wailing and travailing. And yet the Bible says,

And at midnight Paul and Silas prayed, and sang praises unto God: and the prisoners heard them.
Acts 16:25

If you look at this verse in the Greek language, the word translated *heard* literally means that the other prisoners were listening intently to every word Paul and Silas sang. Their words penetrated them. And I don't believe they were singing for God to deliver them, though that wouldn't have been wrong. Paul and Silas were worshipping God because they really were in love with God! They were just loving God and thanking Him for His goodness. That's powerful!

I want to be a person who praises God, not just because it gets me something or gets me out of difficult circumstances; I want to praise Him just because I truly love Him.

This is pure Christianity. I believe this is the reason they were delivered from the situation. If you read Acts

16:26-32, you'll learn that an earthquake came and shook all the prisoners' chains off and opened all the doors. The jailer, thinking everyone had escaped on his watch, was going to kill himself rather than face the consequences. Now, if Paul and Silas had been singing to God just for Him to deliver them, they would have escaped. But Paul told the jailer that he and Silas had not tried to escape nor had any of the other prisoners. That's so powerful! Then the jailer got so convicted that he ended up getting saved and baptized along with his entire household.

You see, when you simply minister to the Lord, miraculous things begin to happen. You're blessing the Lord, but He will never let you out-give Him.

Chapter 6

Stories of Blessing the Lord

When Jamie and I first got started in the ministry, it seemed that people stayed away from our meetings by the thousands. If I had been looking only at physical circumstances and the results I was getting, I would have been discouraged. But the way I coped with it was by focusing on the Lord. I just loved and fellowshipped with Him. Even when I couldn't see things working the way I wanted, I knew I could always have a great relationship with Him. I could always feel like I was pleasing to God. When you understand this, you'll begin to prioritize your relationship with Him, no matter what your circumstances are.

Freer While Imprisoned

Long before I was on television, I was ministering on this very subject through my radio program, and I got a letter from a woman who was in prison for murder. It was three or four pages long. She told me the story of what she had done, and that she had been born again while imprisoned. Nevertheless, her situation was bleak: She was in solitary confinement, her food was slid to her under a door, and she couldn't even go out to exercise. Nobody ever came to visit her, and she had no one to share her faith with. She felt like a drain on society because she was costing taxpayers to feed and keep her alive when all she'd ever done was hurt people.

Then this woman explained that she'd heard me on the radio talking about how God has a need, that He created us for His pleasure. When I got to this part of her letter, I could see where her tears had made the ink run. She said it was the most liberating revelation she had ever received. She now had a purpose for her existence! She wrote, "I'm the only one in this cell, and yet God is here. When I tell Him 'Thank You' and that I appreciate His love for me, I know it ministers to Him. This woman was freer than most people who aren't in prison! Most people are stuck in a routine of endless doing, not knowing how they can bless God. But when you understand that you were made for His pleasure, it will transform you!

"Bless You, Dad"

What does it mean to bless the Lord? For some, it's become a religious cliché to quote scriptures like "*I will bless the Lord at all times*" (Ps. 34:1), but just uttering the words may or may not bless Him.

When my kids were young, I took them and two of their friends for an all-day outing. We rode horses, played in a creek, and ate junk food. If my wife had been with us, she never would have approved of all those things. At the end of the day, we were all filthy dirty. It was a great day! After I got my kids cleaned up, we had a time of devotion, and I prayed with them and put them to bed. After I kissed Peter goodnight and turned out the light, he said, "Dad? You're a good dad." You know what, that blessed me! It made me want to run over, snatch him out of that bed, and do the day all over again.

Now, notice my son didn't say, "Bless you, dad." Sure, those are good words, but they wouldn't have expressed his heart in the same way. The Scripture says, "*Bless the Lord, O my soul*" (Ps. 103:1). That means it needs to come from within you, your heart. When you thank God and name what He's done for you, it blesses Him.

I want to encourage you to stop believing the lie that you have nothing to give God. Again, He inhabits your praises (Ps. 22:3). Just like when my son blessed me and I wanted to bless him even more, I believe that when you start praising God, He wants to do the same for you. As I said in the previous chapter, you cannot out-give Him.

For you to have the relationship with the Lord that He really wants to have with you, you must understand how your praise affects Him. Yes, it affects you, and it affects the devil, but most importantly, it builds relationship with God.

God Rejoices Over You

God is passionate about you. He is excited about you. The average Christian does not have this understanding. But the Scripture says,

> *The LORD thy God in the midst of thee* is *mighty; he will save, he will rejoice over thee with joy; he will rest in his love, he will joy over thee with singing.*
> Zephaniah 3:17

One of the Hebrew words for joy in this verse means to dance and to twirl. I remember when we had a little ministry in Seagoville, Texas, we would just worship the Lord. One time, as we were singing, Jamie had a vision of angels dancing and twirling and spinning all over the place. At that time, she had never read Zephaniah 3:17. She just spoke what she saw. It was an amazing confirmation! So, God doesn't rejoice over us figuratively; He does it literally. This is how He feels about us. That's powerful!

Conclusion

I introduced this booklet by saying that your level of praise reflects how spiritually healthy you are. If you don't have strength, if the devil is running wild in your life, if you don't feel close to the Lord, you are not entering into praise enough.

Praise ought to be a huge part of your relationship with God. Your prayer life ought to be 90 to 95 percent praise and the other 5 to 10 percent asking for things and interceding for other people. For the average person, it's the exact opposite. If you were to spend more time worshiping and loving God, you would discover that you don't have as many needs. It would totally change your perspective. Your desires would even change. You wouldn't crave the things that the world goes after.

I'm inviting you to get so plugged into God that it wouldn't matter whether everything is going the way you'd like it to go. You would realize that God is still real; He hasn't fallen off His throne because things aren't working out for you. As a matter of fact, praise will be the catalyst to get you out of your problems, as it did for Paul and Silas when they were in prison (Acts 16:23-26). This is the way that I live. I constantly praise and thank God for how good He is to me. That doesn't mean I don't have any problems. I've just learned to praise the Lord no matter what I'm going through. Because of the way God has come through for me in the past, I know He's going to be faithful in the future. It shrinks my problems down to where they're no big deal. I know that He will do the same for you. So, I encourage you . . .

> *O magnify the LORD with me, and let us exalt his name together.*
>
> Psalm 34:3

FURTHER STUDY

If you enjoyed this booklet and would like to learn more about some of the things I've shared, I suggest my teachings:

1. *A Better Way to Pray*
2. *God Wants You Well*
3. *The True Nature of God*
4. *You've Already Got It!*

These teachings are available free of charge at **awmi.net** or for purchase at **awmi.net/store**.

Go deeper in your relationship with God by browsing all of Andrew's free teachings.

Receive Jesus as Your Savior

Choosing to receive Jesus Christ as your Lord and Savior is the most important decision you'll ever make!

God's Word promises, *"That if thou shalt confess with thy mouth the Lord Jesus, and shalt believe in thine heart that God hath raised him from the dead, thou shalt be saved. For with the heart man believeth unto righteousness; and with the mouth confession is made unto salvation"* (Rom. 10:9–10). *"For whosoever shall call upon the name of the Lord shall be saved"* (Rom. 10:13). By His grace, God has already done everything to provide salvation. Your part is simply to believe and receive.

Pray out loud: "Jesus, I acknowledge that I've sinned and need to receive what you did for the forgiveness of my sins. I confess that You are my Lord and Savior. I believe in my heart that God raised You from the dead. By faith in

Your Word, I receive salvation now. Thank You for saving me."

The very moment you commit your life to Jesus Christ, the truth of His Word instantly comes to pass in your spirit. Now that you're born again, there's a brand-new you!

Please contact us and let us know that you've prayed to receive Jesus as your Savior. We'd like to send you some free materials to help you on your new journey. Call our Helpline: **719-635-1111** (available 24 hours a day, seven days a week) to speak to a staff member who is here to help you understand and grow in your new relationship with the Lord.

Welcome to your new life!

Receive the Holy Spirit

As His child, your loving heavenly Father wants to give you the supernatural power you need to live a new life. *"For every one that asketh receiveth; and he that seeketh findeth; and to him that knocketh it shall be opened…how much more shall* your *heavenly Father give the Holy Spirit to them that ask him?"* (Luke 11:10–13).

All you have to do is ask, believe, and receive!

Pray this: "Father, I recognize my need for Your power to live a new life. Please fill me with Your Holy Spirit. By faith, I receive it right now. Thank You for baptizing me. Holy Spirit, You are welcome in my life."

Some syllables from a language you don't recognize will rise up from your heart to your mouth (1 Cor. 14:14). As you speak them out loud by faith, you're releasing God's power from within and building yourself up in the spirit

(1 Cor. 14:4). You can do this whenever and wherever you like.

It doesn't really matter whether you felt anything or not when you prayed to receive the Lord and His Spirit. If you believed in your heart that you received, then God's Word promises you did. *"Therefore I say unto you, What things soever ye desire, when ye pray, believe that ye receive* them, *and ye shall have* them" (Mark 11:24). God always honors His Word—believe it!

We would like to rejoice with you, pray with you, and answer any questions to help you understand more fully what has taken place in your life!

Please contact us to let us know that you've prayed to be filled with the Holy Spirit and to request the book *The New You & the Holy Spirit*. This book will explain in more detail about the benefits of being filled with the Holy Spirit and speaking in tongues. Call our Helpline: **719-635-1111** (available 24 hours a day, seven days a week).

Call for Prayer

If you need prayer for any reason, you can call our Helpline, 24 hours a day, seven days a week at **719-635-1111**. A trained prayer minister will answer your call and pray with you.

Every day, we receive testimonies of healings and other miracles from our Helpline, and we are ministering God's nearly-too-good-to-be-true message of the Gospel to more people than ever. So, I encourage you to call today!

About the Author

Andrew Wommack's life was forever changed the moment he encountered the supernatural love of God on March 23, 1968. As a renowned Bible teacher and author, Andrew has made it his mission to change the way the world sees God.

Andrew's vision is to go as far and deep with the Gospel as possible. His message goes far through the *Gospel Truth* television program, which is available to over half the world's population. The message goes deep through discipleship at Charis Bible College, headquartered in Woodland Park, Colorado. Founded in 1994, Charis has campuses across the United States and around the globe.

Andrew also has an extensive library of teaching materials in print, audio, and video. More than 200,000 hours of free teachings can be accessed at **awmi.net**.

Contact Information

Andrew Wommack Ministries, Inc.

PO Box 3333
Colorado Springs, CO 80934-3333
info@awmi.net
awmi.net

Helpline: 719-635-1111 (available 24/7)

Charis Bible College

info@charisbiblecollege.org
844-360-9577
CharisBibleCollege.org

For a complete list of all of our offices,
visit **awmi.net/contact-us**.

Connect with us on social media.

Printed in Dunstable, United Kingdom